THE NAKED EYE

The Naked Eye

By Undra' Ware Sr.

ISBN: 978-0-9980012-1-0

I dedicate this book to my kids—Undra Jr., Jimeyah, and Jamal. Life can be distracting, particularly when you're trying to be yourself in a cruel, judgmental, and unforgiving world.

At times it probably appeared that I wasn't available emotionally and physically, but I did my best as a father with what life had given me. I prayed for your safety daily, ensured that your needs were met, and made myself available, in my opinion. Throughout your lives I tried being a role model, even during my darkest moments. I love each of you differently but yet the same. Each one of your needs was different as I attempted to rise to the challenge of fatherhood.

If I failed in any way, I apologize, and I'm truly sorry. All I want is for each of you to prosper and be productive citizens. I am not perfect, just human.

Love
Dad

To my wife, Angela, words can't explain my behavior or mood swings throughout our marriage. We both know that in the beginning of our marriage I was immature as I struggled to be a loving husband. Although marriage isn't my strong suit, as I'll tell anyone, I truly believe being married saved me from disease, bastard kids, and self-destruction. For that I am forever appreciative that God placed you in my life as my wife.

Contents

CHAPTER 1

Voices of the Heart

"**V**oices of the Heart" stems from relationship trials and errors. Whether relational to family or various friends, we experience heartbreaks as well as disappointments. Perhaps this leads us to questioning their motives in addition to our own as we grow and mature. Dealing with humanity or society, depending on our perspectives and our paths in life, we question (or should question) situations that affect our hearts—dealing with lies and deceit, understanding and appreciating true friendship, as well as truly forgiving.

To be free, one must be willing to be vulnerable.

With Lots of Love

Love is in the air, so don't despair. When the rivers are overwhelming, I'll be there.

Our love has transcended to an even peak; I'm glad it's you I've longed to seek.

My love is like a flower, craving for your shower which makes my heart bloom like a silver spoon.

Being with you makes life worthwhile; just keep being yourself, and never change your style.

Missing You

I plan not to cry as I say goodbye. Embellishing the times we shared and the talks we had will be engraved in my memory and tattooed to my heart, reminding me that you are always near.

The laughter seen and the unconditional love I feel, would be a tomb carried within my life, as I cherish your kindred spirit, which created a declaration of family that will not perish.

Your strength of metal taught me to be strong, even when faced with adversity. Your childlike ways resembled a feather, so light but free in being yourself regardless of those who ridiculed you through friendship or as enemies.

Mostly, you taught me to appreciate a grandfather's love, warmth, concern, protection, wisdom, and a sense of family.

Goodbye

Saying goodbye is so hard to do, especially when my heart has feelings for you.

It began so fast, untouched about how long it would last.

We pulled and tugged, wearing each other down, our hearts filled with joy because of what we've found.

Saying goodbye isn't easy to do; it makes your heart ache and feel very blue.

A love that was lost and now is found—you will always be my jewel, my crown.

It was nothing we did or anything we said; reality is just hitting me upside my head.

First love we are and that we will be, forever eternally.

So look up and reach for a star. Though we are far, our love for each other is branded like a scar.

Friendship

Friendship is the general article from the heart, and in most cases, it never departs. Some friends are new and show they care, but friends from the past are always there.

Friendship has a price that one must pay; it's the one who never leaves your side or leads you to stray. It stems from trust, honesty, and respect; it's not like a card game when you pull from a deck.

A friend is one who listens, never judges, and truly understands; thank God there's no competition in getting the upper hand.

Through our trials and struggles, it is only a few who care; that is why through our friendship, we draw near.

Untitled

—∞∞∞—

Although we're apart in more ways than one, I can still recall how we had fun.

Our conversation always had meaning; though time has passed, I know that I'm still clinging.

Maturity has truly set in as I continue to think about you, my friend. I've learned that emotions never die while continually asking myself, "Why?"

Those moments we shared were intimate to me as you touched and captured my heart, soul, and spirituality.

Your smile, joy, and sincerity are something I will always treasure; they were worth more than gold, and that's what I treasured.

Life went on as I watched you grow, but let me share this last thing that you should know, as time went by, I now understand why.

The thought of you transcends my loneliness to a sweet array of aromatic roses, dripped in morning dew, reflecting images of a rainbow.

Forgiveness

⁓

Forgiveness is something that's hard to do; we search all around but still remain blue.

The heart is filled with so much pain as the harsh reality still remains.

We hear the voice of hope as we seek to heal, but only this paper cut is all I can feel.

Though I ride the tides of life, waiting and wanting to let go, in given time, I'll relieve this strife; but until then I must spiritually grow.

Shall We Dance?

You're as cute as you can be, as your smile is tempting me. Your persona reflects rose petals dripping with dew; I can only think of getting with you.

A friendly greeting keeps me looking forward to our meetings; though we don't see each other much, I long for your touch.

Sensations are near when you're around me, my dear, stimulating my mind as I'm curious to what I'll find.

Feelings run deep, and this we know; my only question is, How far will it go?

You truly are a star that gleams in the night; let me guide you to ecstasy as we dance in the light.

Untitled

Caught in a whirl of swarming emotions, confusion plagues the intellect as if various channels are malfunctioned. What shall I do? I hold on to my true identity, but deceit was sweet as cherries. I sit in a daze, questioning and wondering, day in and day out. If this is love, then I see why people go crazy.

A strong emotion that takes control and leaves you weak mentally and physically. A fear of being hurt as well as embarrassed. A feeling of guilt and of course happiness. How can one word possess such power, which seems to last forever unless the flames somehow deteriorate?

The power of love has no boundaries; it's like a special medicine many try to find, but once at hand, it will make you blind. If by chance you stumble upon a shaky path that twirls you about, don't be afraid. It's only love; that's how you'll know not to reroute.

CHAPTER 2

Family

In my life, family was truly an inspiration and foundation. The death of both grandmothers motivated me to be my best, as I wrestled with my inner demons while discovering myself. Traveling south every summer was significant in my childhood. Hanging out with family and friends and just getting away from the city was refreshing. Although the southern heat was scorching, going south to my southern roots was enlightening. Life was different and difficult, but I learned to persevere and embrace family—family unity, additions to the clan, good food, and lots of love.

No family is perfect, but embrace what you have. Love unconditionally.

Family Reunion

We come together for this occasion, meeting each other for the first or countless times; there have been many additions as we continue to carry out our family traditions.

Greeting and hugging one another with a smile has always been our style.

Filling one with warmth, love, and history is what it's all about; instilling a sense of family that the younger generation will not be without.

Acknowledging God in our way is truly ingrained in the black family as it never goes astray.

That's why we are here, to show our children that God and family is sincere.

A Grandmother's Love

A grandmother's love runs like a waterfall, forever providing nutrients in sustaining life. The nutrients of love, empathy, sharing, and forgiveness-just to name a few.

Grandma, your life reflected the characteristics of Christ. As a child, I observed how you fed the hungry, encouraged the weak in heart, and loved strangers as if they were your own.

Although Grandma wasn't college educated, she always stated, "Living and experiencing life was my education." Through God's strength, she persevered through the Great Depression, endured the Civil Rights Movement, and over-came Jim Crow.

God also allowed her to witness presidents such as Kennedy, Nixon, Carter, Clinton, Bush, and now Barack Obama, the first African American president of the United States. Most importantly, she raised, nurtured, educated, and loved all her children.

Grandma, I thank God for you and the values of family and love that's embedded in my spirit and heart. You exemplified the true meaning of following Christ through your life work.

Rest in peace. Your grandson, Undra.

Family

———⊛———

Whether through bloodlines or the bonding between friends, the family should stand like a pyramid at its highest point not swaying or threatening to fade. Standing strong while enduring the storms will aid in overcoming fear and if one should cry, there should always be someone there to wipe your eye.

The unity of family should exclude loose ends, while coming to a merge of forgiveness and togetherness while bonding at the base causing an upward mobility of faith, love, and respect. We are what we are taught. If we're taught distress, there will be no rest; if we're taught to fight, that will be our plight.

No family is alike; each bears their own shame. Some may hold their guilt as well as their pain, but we must overcome our faults. Seek the truth and do not resort to the blame game. That goes for you and even me, so as you can see, no one is free.

Family is real for it sustains our existence as well as our identity. Sometimes you may feel unloved or unwanted; the reality is every family has issues. Be man or woman enough to drop your pride and make sure it's not you.

The Children

I yearn to be heard, I yearn to be loved, and the innocence that bathes me is equivalent to a dove.

I learn what I see and this is true; if you don't believe me, just look around you.

I depend on you to show me the way, but I must warn you, God will penalize you if you lead me astray.

My mind is filled with dreams and possibilities, but who is honorable enough to teach with such credibility?

I am in the image of the one who creates, so guide and mold my mind as you dare to educate.

Thanksgiving

—◦◦◦—

Thanksgiving was all live, no family drama or any jive. The family got together showing lots of love; there was nothing but peace and the heavenly dove.

The food was good from head to toe, people eating seconds and thirds wanting mo, mo, and mo. There is much laughter and rooms filled with joy, people leaning back holding their bellies saying, "Oh, boy."

Both generations, young and old, bonding their spirits and minds as never before. No one showed conflict or war as they walked in or out the door.

As the feast came to an end, tears of anticipation began. No one wants to say goodbye while others started to cry.

For some, this was their first gathering, and for a few it might be their last, but one thing's for sure, this Thanksgiving was a blast.

A Friend

When I'm in need, you're there indeed. Through my valley lows and woes; through thick and thin, you are truly my friend.

You were there through my sickness as well as my weakness. Showing concern, compassion, and understanding in a way that a friend can do. Thanks for being real but mostly for being you.

We walk different paths while sharing our experiences, finding humor where there is pain; acknowledging and observing our growth through the storms of life as we endure what remains.

Although we don't agree on how life should be, we respect each other enough to let ourselves be free.

CHAPTER 3

Encouragement

During this time, I was experiencing darkness in my life. Being used by people, having no hope and began questioning my faith. I think we waste so much time making excuses and pointing fingers that we lose focus on what's really important. Selfishness becomes a norm while we witness the pain of one another.

Once we learn to utilize our time to display empathy and love, then perhaps we can be on a path of upward mobility within society and ourselves.

Untitled

—∞∞∞—

To live in a coldhearted world, we must first know God as well as ourselves.

You must have faith as you walk alone in darkness and hope that you'll see the light.

To live is experiencing the good and bad, which helps us mature and become stronger mentally and spiritually.

Life is an opportunity that revolves around negative and positive situations; each individual has their own path to salvation.

Due to different beliefs and various timeframes, some people have developed fears and learned to say no, but when you have your own dreams, there is a path you must go.

Time is everyone's enemy, so don't delay; people are always negative or positive but go on with your life and continue to pray.

Untitled

Be true to yourself and let your light shine, in which the world will know that you are mine.

The trial is not easy but always do your best, and keep in mind that it's all a spiritual test.

Though the road may be bare and it appears you are alone, it is God whom you seek as he makes you strong.

The world will see that God truly exists because he will prevail throughout our outer midst.

Tribulations we must overcome; let's remind ourselves who's in control and grant the outcome.

FAME

Friends are those who truly care, they're always there to ease your fear. Sometimes they run and may even hide, but that's not an indication of avoiding your side. To be a friend, learn to listen and avoid being judgmental. Understanding this should strengthen friendships to last forever and not go astray.

Advice should be given from the wise, regardless of their age. Advice is given from family and friends, it's up to you to take heed and truly know what you need. Every piece of advice I shared was not to destroy but to build self-esteem and open your eyes to possibilities. If you want something, stop talking and create a plan to make it happen.

Man exists in the world, but how many are truly men? Will a man sacrifice his own needs and wants for others? A man should be sensitive to his woman's needs. What good is a man if he has no cause or purpose of being? I hope you can see I tried to be the best toward my immediate family. Times are hard but I chose you to get the most of me. There is always something wrong in society, but in the decade of the 90's, what's right? Our men are declining for whatever reason, and many children are confused because of this treason.

Essential and excitement is what I add; I apologize if I made you sad. My love for you isn't a joke, so calm your nerves before you get a stroke. I want you to know, my love for you truly shows in what I do and what I say. So I conclude by asking you to stay regardless of my selfish ways.

Stay Strong

—∽∽∽—

Stay strong when things are going wrong, while the tides of life are rocking your boat, don't drown or despair; just stay afloat.

The waves may be overwhelming or a bit too high; just keep the faith and look toward the Heavenly sky. Stay strong when things are going wrong.

Keep striving forward and don't lean back, but always remember it's a spiritual attack. You can achieve if you only believe, just stay strong when things are going wrong.

Black Gospel

Black Gospel, Black Gospel, lift up your eyes, as you can see we've left the African skies.

We've been uprooted to our dismay and replanted across the waters in American clay.

The sound of the drums ring through the air as history reminds us that things are not fair.

Whether it's from the Caribbean or through the oceans and seas, it's like a drug that heals if you truly believe.

The sound of the gospel enhances our lives as our body and soul needs to be revived.

Black Gospel is the truth and will set you free while society wants us to remain in slavery; but while we praise, dance, and sing; the sound of Black Gospel will always ring.

Precious Time

—∞∞∞—

Time is ticking and I don't know what to do. I must be careful or I'll turn blue.

I'm needed over here while wanted over there; life is overwhelming and so unfair.

I try to please those around me but come up short. Thank God this isn't school, or I'd get a bad report.

My days are hurried without much to gain, and my body is tired due to the aches and pains.

Time is ticking as if it's a race; each day is crucial without much to waste, but in the end I just want Grace.

Untitled

As I look over my life, I can see that God has taken care of me. Through my trials I can see the victories that pleased my soul and eased the intellect of self.

Life is good and getting better, though I can't see what the future holds, I know God will make a way. Whether good or bad I will prevail, life goes on as I share this tale.

Though I pray daily and see no change, God will make a way as he arrange. Patience is a virtue and that I know, that's my only downfall as I continue to grow.

Untitled

---∞---

Life is good as you continue to pray but keep your strength and don't be led astray.

Pray to God and not to man but await the miracle as it transcends.

Life is hard, life is good; we can make things happen if you understood.

Don't go here or don't go there, life can be so unfair; but if you pray through thick or thin, this little battle is yours to win.

Excuses

Like Nike says, "Just do it!"

Why make excuses for something you're not going to do, your words and actions are just untrue.

Time will tell about the reality you speak but what you display is an evil streak.

This week it's this and now it's that, if this were a game it would be a zero stat.

Excuses are made for lack of trying or maybe just plain lying. Whatever the case you shouldn't delay that is what causes us to go astray.

Nike says, "Just do it!" Never did it say quit. If we keep making excuses nothing will get done so wipe off that smile because you're not having fun.

Leave the excuses where you can and be strong while taking a stand, life goes on and that we know, spread your wings and allow yourself to grow.

Favors

⸻

Favors are something I truly hate; one way or another there's always a debate.

If anything goes wrong, who's to blame? Or will it become the same old bullshit game?

Who is accountable for what goes down, or would you become bitter and just wear a frown?

Favors are something I don't like to do; in most cases it makes me feel blue. It appears to be true. Your family is always the culprit just as much as you, and the sad part about it, they don't have a clue.

Time Passes

—∞∞∞—

Birth is unique as we engage in life trials and tribulations, being allowed to learn while we grow; taking for granted that time passes. From childhood, most of us were raised to believe in God but as time passes some of us became distraught with materialism and individualism; causing a deterioration of the heart as we make our Earthly depart.

The clock of life ticks ferociously passing through our vigorous youth, which fades diligently as our bones weakens with old age. We must ask ourselves, How am I living within the midst of my precious time? Did you leave laughter, joy, or peace, or were you sowing seeds of strife, strain, or pain?

Regardless, time does pass, and that we know. Keep in mind, it's what you leave behind and how well you've nurtured what you were willing to sow as the future will continue to grow.

CHAPTER 4

Dark Times

So many are dying in our midst; death has become a social norm. In the streets of Chicago, even during the day, you can see the darkness lurking in the streets. We walk like zombies, desensitized to our emotions and rarely concerned about one another. Living among the dead, what a sight to see.

Principalities of good and evil are truly in this land; we see this every day, or are some of us just numbed?

Homecoming

—⁂—

A homecoming for most is well deserved as our life story remain preserved.

Our family on earth must understand and prepare for this departure as our heavenly Father joins our heart.

Take this time to reflect over your life and ask God to remove any strife, because one day you too will be coming home.

Untitled

—⊶⊷⊶—

Why must we succumb to this, watching the violence within our midst?

Pain and sorrow is what we engage causing our families to live with rage.

Our society is filled with guilt and shame but don't point the finger because we are to blame. Our children are hurting and that we see, thanks to drugs and guns as well as you and me.

We failed to love and give them hope as their world becomes filled with dope. We failed to teach them the value of life as our communities encounter the various strife. We took them away from God and that wasn't a good thing to do; that is self-evident because this tragedy could have happened to you. The church gave them the way, now the Devil lurks as they're being led astray.

We the people must be in tuned, we cannot wait and it must be soon.

Stricter gun laws must be passed or I can assure you this funeral will not be the last.

The streets must be safe and we must do our part, if we don't act now when will it start?

CHAPTER 5

Community

A lot is happening in the community; whether good or bad, it affects us collectively and individually. Sitting in a coffee shop discussing issues of the day or just existing as the years pass away. Events that stain our memories and become part of our history—I raise the question, where were you?

Living life just isn't good enough; reach for the stars and leave your mark.

Untitled

—ᴄᴇᴇᴏ—

Another year has come and gone, there was a lot to learn as I write this song.

Being involved takes a lot, it starts as fun and ends as not.

Let me explain what I decided to do, while you determine whether it's true.

Going to school takes so much time, I'm trying my best not to lose my mind; perhaps that's why I'm writing this rhyme.

Politics affects us every day, I got involved hoping to pave my way. All I see is dishonesty, people expecting loyalty and the lack of unity. Internally, I raise the question of integrity.

It takes responsibility and patience too, I later discovered how people depend on you. They use you up and leave you dry, I ask myself, why-why-why?

Some may lie while others persuade, causing the true agenda to be delayed.

Being of service can cause much pain but I can't stop now due to the knowledge I gained, I only pray that my work isn't in vain.

Another year has come and gone, there was a lot to learn as I write this song.

Westside Coffee Express

———— ⊶⊷⊶ ————

A relaxing café is where you ought to be, in order to ease your mind and escape reality.

As you enter our door, the smell of sweet mist lingers in the air, awakening your senses as we greet you kindly, while showing that we care.

You have the choice of selecting the beans as we grind them right, to start your day not being uptight.

The beans are brewed with love as you await the taste. We aim to please and make sure nothing goes to waste.

We provide peace, harmony, and intellect too. But everything we provide will depend on you.

Year 2001

As we enter 2001, we need to ask ourselves what have we done?

Our world has consumed so much fear that hatred, greed, and jealousy is always near.

Our children are suffering with so much pain but the world doesn't care due to selfish gain.

Most of us want to be wealthy as we risk our lives and become unhealthy.

As children of God, we should resist the nonsense that exists. Understand that life is short and when it ends, there will be a report.

The question is, what have you done?

Through your education, title, or faith, who did you help along the way or did you cause them to go astray?

As children of God, we must do our best and remember it's all a spiritual test.

911

―∞―

September 11th has lived up to what it's to be, a State of Emergency. Since that day nothing has been the same, people ran to church trying to save their name. People have spied and lied while others have cried and died. We must get out and vote before we let this slide.

Our world is full of hatred and death that consumes us in a coffin. We are witnessing human sacrifices and bombs galore, the world isn't safe for us anymore due to death knocking at our door.

Our so-called leaders are creating havoc and fear, we walk out our homes with suspicion of those who are near.

Terror has become a new age epidemic as each bomb explodes, it remains to mimic. I point at you, you point at me but in the end there's nowhere to flee. Bam and boom the world is doomed.

Yes, the world is truly a State of Emergency; 911.

World-Class

—⦿—

World-Class Service symbolizes caring for human needs and concerns.

We are here to serve customers as well as one another, that's why you are considered my brother.

For every pain or even sorrow, we can call the Department of Human Services for a better tomorrow.

Each need isn't the same, it's not up to us to determine who's to blame, just give common courtesy with a smile and your name.

World-Class Service isn't an easy task, it calls for a unique person that doesn't wear a mask.

So when you think of service it is a pleasant delight, never answer the phone being uptight.

Serve with a smile and a pleasant voice, know that you did your best as you obtain God's zest.

In the end, World-Class Service will truly withstand because you did your best in serving your fellow man.

44th President

History, history for the world to see, we've elected a black President that can relate to me.

Tears of joy flow through the world as we observe President Barack Obama as America's first black pearl. He's the President of this land; let's thank God for this miracle and this man.

He reigns over America, the nation that once enslaved and tortured our ancestors of the past. Presently, each generation should seize this moment as we shout and dance throughout the land, "at last, at last."

America witnessed history on November 4, 2008, the weather was great. Seventy degrees in Chicagoland, it should have been cold but Barack was the man. The world was watching and waiting, anticipating something great. It happened, Barack Obama became the 44th President of the United States.

The spirit of our ancestors sifted through the air as the doors of Heaven poured out its blessing everywhere. I recalled the scripture, "the first shall be last and the last shall be first."

M.L.K.

⸺⸻⸺

The dreamer, Dr. King was a man of God. He stood against adversity and faced his foes with conviction. Dr. King's methodology wasn't just focused on Civil Rights and equality but for humanity to learn how to accept each other's value systems and beliefs. He showed us how to overcome fears of racial bias and to see the good of a man's heart and soul. Value what we gain together in love and discard hatred.

We must teach our children the value of their history and ancestry regardless of the negative imprint America imposed on us. Engage ourselves to be of service whether within the community, academia, or civic life. Remember, the problems we faced yesterday and today are not individual but as a collective whole.

Crime, poverty, and education disparity are social ills that destroy our community due to lack of jobs and concern for humanity.

CHAPTER 6

Social Justice

"Social Justice" came about from observing injustice within America. Black youth being killed within inner cities, lack of love and respect among African Americans, black communities leaning on black leaders in government instead of engaging among themselves toward resolutions. History seems to repeat itself, but I don't understand why—we're more educated, some of us have more economic power, but we seem to lack something.

Love and respect yourself first; then others will soon follow.

Lies and Deceit

As time surpasses us, history seems to repeat itself. I raised the question whether it's lies or deceit.

As children, we are taught to be honest and don't lie. Somewhere in our adult lives, we deter from this belief of truth and walk in the obsession of lies and deceit. For example, Corporate America is filled with greedy and dishonest people. Those who have the money and power will do anything to keep it in comparison with those who are not corrupted and wait patiently for their opportunity. It's relative to that flashy drug dealer in your neighborhood convincing your kids that this is the dream of getting rich.

Is It A Lie or Deceit?

They say America is the land of opportunity. With all creeds of people, America should be a river of honey. But racism and separation plague America. Sure, it may be the land of opportunity but for whom? Everything seems to be a black and white issue which excludes the rights for blacks or should I say opportunity. Sure, there are a few among many who make it but what about the unmentioned 60 percent? Since we are a nation of all creeds, everything can't be black or white.

Is It A Lie or Deceit?

We should open our minds and eyes to the truth. Not one culture has superiority over another. Diversity is what makes a nation along with understanding and overlooking your fears to strengthen a nation.

B.P.C.

Black Power Convention

1. We are part of a nation that no one is familiar with.

2. We are what we stand to be and nothing less.

3. In society, we stand high but sit very low.

4. We have the understanding and experience but little knowledge.

5. We must lean forward and pull together, for there is power as one.

6. We are a great multitude but few are strengthened. Courage is within but many are weak.

7. If we come together we can defeat our opposers.

8. God is our creator and there is nothing we can't overcome.

We Shall Rise

⸺⸙⸺

We shall rise, we shall rise like a raging tidal wave gulping everything in our path. There will be no stopping us as we migrate forward through the wrath.

Our story will be told throughout the years how our people shed more than just tears. We left the shores of Africa and boarded ships as slaves but that was just the beginning of new ground we were about to graze.

Endurance was a test we had to embrace as we entered America as the Negro race. We overcame obstacles to our dismay but it was our spirit that guided us to pray.

Bonding like a nucleus that we can be; years passed and they banned slavery.

Doors began to open as we prevailed, while our white counterparts should have exhaled. We became educated and began to soar; some of us became doctors, lawyers, teachers and a whole lot more. Sports, politics, and entertainment are our way to fame but as we continue let's not forget God's name.

POWER

The principle of mankind is to love and unite, but how can we rise if we continue to fight? Our perspective should be to abolish black-on-black enslavement as a priority in humanity. People live to progress, but we halt our own and cause many to regress.

Our vocabulary should change from oneself to ourselves as a people. Looking back in time, unification paved the way; since we've become educated most of us have gone astray. Ignorant with selfish needs, we tend to forget elevation is nice but on our descent there will be a price. Reaching the top is every man's goal, but without a strong chain, there is no gain. Keep in mind, united we stand and divided we shall fall.

Wisdom is a characteristic that few of us show but when activated the whole world will know. Wisdom is the key to life, so why do we live in so much strife? To unify as a people shows knowledge and understanding of our purpose and state of being. Catering to human needs is a must as we rebuild our trust.

Something essential has always been a part of our culture. Unification should be our dedication and continue to let our love flow. Change is what we need; dispose of our selfishness, envy and greed. In order for our purpose to be complete, black-on-black violence must retreat.

Our reward is peace and happiness as we rise in the light; our fear is over because we learned to unite. No one individual has the light, but a multitude will always glow as we combine our knowledge and wisdom to let it all grow.

Running out of Time

Time marches on; it never stands like a rock. Its days are full of events affecting our existence. Life, death, happiness, or pain; time marches on and never stays the same.

It spreads like the endless waters surrounding our Earth's atmosphere running the course like a golfer. Just like the sunshine as far-east and it never fails to set in the west, giving us a different glimpse of time. Yes, time marches on and never stands still but turns just like a wheel.

We as a culture or people symbolize time. Most of us flow evenly balancing time like nature, while many of us rant wildly never to catch up wishing we could. Yes, time truly marches on leaving us running out of time.

It passes leaving us like statues of dust yearning and thirsting for a second or even a minute only to do nothing. Yes, time marches on with much to gain and nothing to lose, but it is up to us to choose.

Untitled

— ∞ —

The implementation of Black Codes and Jim Crow is alive and true today.

Fear allows one to be dictated to, oppressed, and conditioned. When the oppressed get sick and tired of being oppressed, then they began to exercise their rights. The movement of the oppressed is done incrementally but eventually mobilizes one by one when individuals unite and resist the status quo. The status quo of lies, abuse, unfair treatment, harassment, and misconduct is what our ancestors endured throughout slavery.

Jesus overcame these obstacles during Roman oppression; it ended in death. Dr. King overcame the plague of southern and northern oppression; it ended in death. Malcolm X sought the truth during his Mecca experience; it ended in death.

Today, this illness still exists. The sheets of the KKK are replaced with corporate greed and control. Managerial staff use work rules to brutally control and intimidate their subordinate staff. The house Negro implement harsh treatment to appeal to Massa. Suspension or threat of termination plagues our weak economy. The job market is so bad, companies look for reasons to harass and terminate employees. So many people unemployed, it's even hard for those with degrees. Lack of healthcare and those who can't afford it are penalized for not having it.

Times are hard; why endure much foolishness?

Poetry

Words that express the inner thoughts of man, whether it's good or bad, we become branded in our minds and souls.

It's the beginning of understanding as we look forward to tomorrow, but keep in mind, it's not promised.

Poetry is a form of written communication, which can be considered documentation for past and future generations. Either way, it exists through factual events or imaginable fantasies that affect us emotionally or spiritually.

Wisdom

———⊷⊶———

Wisdom is the ability to accept others and their differences as they develop and blossom in their own time.

We may say and do things at inappropriate times but that's no reason to judge with our insensitive behavior.

We are all God's children, and with this fact, it's imperative that each of us is allowed to utilize our individual talent as we seek our path to destiny.

My words can be sharp, but I mean no harm. I apologize, but it's important to know; respect goes two ways not just one.

Reality

The past is gone and I can just be me; no more lies to tell because I've been set free.

My rainy days have finally ceased; now I can rest with a little peace.

Life is good, so inhale the air; I just realized some people just don't care. They say they do but really they don't. When it's time to put up, they really won't.

Keeping It Real

—❧—

Keep it real and wear no shame when you get caught in the web of your game. When things go wrong, regardless of how long, don't begin singing that ole sorry song.

No one near to truly care, you created a bed full of fear. Keep it real when the words can't explain and you find yourself trying to maintain. Friends are far and no longer there; you pushed them away and they don't even care. It's a brand-new day as you stray, finding no happiness where you lay.

Keep it real and be true to yourself. Your mind is closed and your heart is stubborn, creating a void because you're not seeking Heaven. Full of pain and rejecting the reality of life; deep within you carry much strife.

Keep it real and acknowledge that it's you living with anger and despair while tasting the bitterness of life and trying to escape the grip of frustration; but to break loose, you must stop your hesitation.

You can't enjoy love being phony to yourself and trying to fool everyone else. Those who keep it real can easily express by not holding on to some unholy mess.

Unison

Unification is what we need; we can't be selfish if we plan to succeed.

Though the smell of distrust is in the air, we must stay focused while trying to be fair.

To remain in the plan, we must understand the need for unison as we continue to stand.

Even though the race is tight, be relaxed and not uptight.

In the end, you can stand tall from enduring the hard labor and winning it all.

Immigration

─❦─

Immigrants, immigrants are everywhere; if you don't be careful they'll soon be there. Illegal they are while determined to stay, they multiply in numbers each and every day.

They are not legal and this we know, so why does our government allow them to grow?

Our rights as citizens have been violated while the government and corporations overlook what's regulated.

Though history was made and this is true, the world was watching as you illegally came through.

Truth

The truth will set you free, although it may tear the heart and even drive lovers or friends apart; it will however free your mind, heart, and soul.

It may bring about respect and revitalize too, as you seek answers that you already knew. Depending on the emotion it may bring, whether up or down, don't stop living or breathing or even hide behind a frown.

Today, truth can be a new beginning. We may think about yesterday, but it's important to look forward to tomorrow's hope and ambition.

Hear and listen to the echoes of forgiveness as you yearn for the dreams of the future. Truth is like a piercing spear seeking the blood of our inequities. However, with time, our wounds will heal only leaving the scars of triumph and victory.

What Have We Done?

We need to stop building on our negative mode of selfishness, envy, jealousy, and greed and follow the spirit so that our brothers and sisters can be freed.

The time has come for us as a people to react to solutions, not upon situations. Prepare ourselves mentally and spiritually for yet another revolution.

What Have We Done?

We must open our eyes and see our people's sorrow for if we don't act now there will be no tomorrow.

The cause for our struggle still remains but our ignorance of the Armageddon is the same.

Our society suffers from drugs, AIDS, and guns but when we hear the news many of us act stunned.

We must act now to preserve our African existence because the future holds no promises for a struggle or a need for existence.

What Have We Done?

No Change

I sit here in this office surrounded by three walls, a window, and a door relating to my incarcerated brothers and sisters. I'm in the workplace being whipped with directives given by a supervisor that looks like me. I am chained to a workstation but can't move unless I receive permission from the overseer. This scenario reminds me of how my ancestors had to endure Jim Crow as well as the Black Codes of yesterday.

It's dangerous observing and encountering this same ideology as I sit in this cell they call an office. Isolation can be good at times, I can hear the voice of God and see the injustice that plagues this environment.

The arrangements are the same: place your scared Negroes with titles over the majority and allow them to demoralize the masses as the slave master rewards them monetarily. They run to their masters like dogs wagging their tails; a rub on the head from Massa soothes them as they return to overseer duties.

Historically, every regime has fallen. In every generation, God rises up a leader to slay this methodology and restore new order. Perhaps mankind should be wiped from the Earth. We haven't learned the true meaning of brotherly love. Apparently, we practice control, hatred, jealousy, and envy just to name a few.

Although my body is entrapped within the confinements of this office, my mind travels back to the past and looks toward the future. I share these words during this time, so my people can see what changed then or even now.

Affirmation

—⊷⊶—

The world is crazy and full of violence, corruption, and lies. It's very difficult being true to yourself especially when faced with adversity.

Bankruptcy, suspensions from jobs, more lies to endure, I don't know how much more I can take. Revival was good, "From Let Go and Let God"; "Take It and Handle It"; but mostly, "It's Over." Stop looking back and remaining stuck, only look back to reflect on the goodness of God.

Friday the thirteenth, 7/13/12, I received another disciplinary packet from the job, just because I felt uncomfortable signing some documents. This attack has been ongoing about four years and escalated after I submitted facts and supporting documents to higher authorities about management not following procedures. State government isn't right. They say you are protected under whistle blower laws, but not for me.

However this 7/13/12 ended on a positive and spiritual note. I was supposed to go out clubbing but I didn't. Instead, I flipped pages through the bible reading various scriptures, I finally became fixed on Romans, Chapter 12 and Verse 1 through 2. After reading scripture, my wife returned home and got comfortable, when she checked her phone, it was open to Galatians, Chapter 1 verse 3 through 5.

We both marveled in this miraculous experience. The timing couldn't have been better. I recall her being happy and fearful as I was grateful that no matter what we were facing in life, this was a reminder that God dwells in our lives.

Mirage

I see people who resemble me but are they truly a reflection of my being?

Their color is of African descent but of a different shade. Some are dark, some are light, and some may even be white.

The hatred of self is rampant. I've experienced the lashings of economic hardship by the hands of those whose ancestors' blood marinated the fields of their oppressor. No more chains but our mind and spirit hold us in bondage to Jim Crow and Black Code Laws of yesterday.

I am convinced, we hate ourselves. We inflict pain instead of love within our culture and community regardless of how God displayed love to us from the beginning.

Oppressors do fall eventually, due to their ignorance and a cold heart. The intentions of the heart seals the fate of the unjust. We should learn from the past, good overcomes evil.

I see people that resemble me but are they truly a reflection of my being?

UJOMA—Unity

Understanding our self-worth and learning to value and love ourselves as a people can lead to a great distribution to humanity.

To achieve justice, stand firm in what you believe and allow your spirit to do what's right. Although you may be faced with adversity, the joy of triumph after trials and tribulations will fulfill its own reward.

Have an open mind and heart to different value systems regardless of ethnic differences and clashes. Be observant in all you do and especially who and what is around you.

Money is universal, use it wisely but don't worship it. Money should be used for building humanity not destroying or dominating lives.

Adjust our mindset for the building of God's Kingdom. Activate your heart and achieve your dreams. Keep a positive attitude and assist those you can.

UJOMA—The principle of UJOMA is within all of us; it's a practice that takes discipline and a sincere heart to bring forth its fruit.

What's Going On?

⸺ ⚭ ⸺

Marvin Gaye asked the question, "What's Going On?" Nothin but the same old game. Emmitt Till, black male, was murdered for flirting with a white woman in August 1955 and today Trayvon Martin, black male, was killed by a Latino male for wearing a hoody as he walked home with candy, Skittles, in his hand, February 2012.

What's Going On?

Our ancestors endured the great depression of years past: lack of jobs, unilateral education, and inadequate housing that plagues us today in 2012. Financial institutions get a bailout as foreclosures is at an all-time high, unemployment rate hasn't improved due to lack of skills and political propaganda.

What's Going On?

Our leaders of yesterday probably died in vain, King risked his life for a better future that only mirrors a dream. Malcolm was enlightened but was cut short due to jealousy and envy. Our people remain afflicted with self-hate instead of love. We sell each other out instead of building our image of the great pyramids that exists throughout time.

Marvin, you ask, "What's going on?" Nothing but the same. Our people suffer from imprisonment of their mind. They are free but remain in slavery. No more protest, just accepting the status quo. Doing what's right and standing for justice has become devalued as Uncle Tom Negroes now carry the whip of the oppressor.

Black Codes are replaced with rules and regulations and enforced with directives to break the will and spirit of a man. What's Going On? Nothing but the same. Different era and players but the same old game.

The Methodology of Control!

Unity

Unification is oneness with ourselves and accepting others regardless of their ethnicity, religious beliefs, and values. It's the combining of one goal and purpose for a particular cause.

From a humanitarian perspective, it's imperative that we address societal issues of gun violence, healthcare, and lack of jobs within our community. We must become engaged just like our ancestors and Jesus.

Ignorance can no longer be our excuse. We must become leaders as God has called us to be by utilizing our resources such as schools, libraries, internet, and of course the church. Our kids are hurting and have no hope for tomorrow or even value life. We as parents have failed but it's not too late to create change in our neighborhoods.

With love and enough effort, we can come together in unity and stop the violence within our community. It starts with you! Overcome your fears, exercise your faith and belief in God, and display love for one another.

CHAPTER 7

A Realm Revealed through the Naked Eye

I contemplated for many years whether or not to share these particular experiences. To some they may appear to be unrealistic, while others may be able to relate due to their spiritual growth or understanding. Nevertheless I am compelled to share and perhaps free those unbelievers, while sustaining those in the faith. At this moment in time, we are experiencing a historic and global pandemic called Coronavirus. Social distancing has become a new social order as many are dying. Whether a human mistake or spiritual punishment, we are witnessing something unorthodox in our time.

We live in a physical world that is seen by sight, but we overlook or deny the spiritual existence among us and fail to walk in the light.

Mountaintop (Calling)

This experience—as I gather my thoughts—scares me. Every time I think of Jesus and his calling of the disciples, I think it was honorable but devastating. As I share my encounter, I recall the timeframe—if I'm not mistaken, this spiritual revelation happened in 1986. Around this time I was employed at Harris Bank and then terminated. I was accused of stealing a stock certificate, which eventually was found on the floor near a coworker's desk. While working at this establishment, I had a female boss who almost never engaged in a civilized conversation with me, and when she did, always did so in a negative tone.

Getting back to my point: In my opinion, the calling from Jesus is different for every individual. In my case, my girlfriend Angie and I were residing at 81st and Maryland, in a first floor apartment. This was our first apartment— two young African Americans, and it was pretty nice and cozy but had some negativity. The kitchen always stayed cold, unless heated by the oven, and the dining room had a chandelier that wasn't modern; maybe it was from the '40s or '50s.

Well, it was in this apartment that I experienced Satan and God. The dream or vision happened in three parts. The first vision was filled with night, nothing around, just the sound of death and no view—darkness! It reminded me of a cave beneath the Earth's surface or perhaps its center. I recall a deep and pointed mountain as I heard a voice acknowledging and complimenting me on my watch. I was baffled. I thought, *Who would acknowledge my watch in a place like this?*

I was cordial before replying, "Thanks." I remember going in and out of sleep, because I relayed each conversation to Angie as if she were witness to this experience.

In the next part of this dream, I ended up on a mountaintop. It was beautiful, and there was much to see. I heard a voice saying, "You can have all this if you come down." Now, I'm not crazy, but the only way down was in this red sled. The elevation was too great to be foolish. I replied, "If I have to go down, I'll find another way."

The third part was like a recital. Every sentence that was said, I repeated back to Angie. The voice was clear and calm as it said, "You have a gift, you are chosen, and go tell the people." I never shared this with anyone other than my immediate family. I don't talk about it, but I think about it every once in a while. I've got to be honest, when I heard *go tell the people,* I immediately awoke and asked Angie, "Are you talking to me in my sleep?" I didn't fall back asleep due to fear. Angie and I talked for a while until the alarm clock sounded.

Now that I'm older and reflect back on these spiritual experiences, I see how God interacts with us or me through the spiritual realm. As I reflect on the first part of the dream, I see Satan wanted my time and soul. That's why my watch was significant.

Being on the mountain was memorable. I thought about Dr. King as he expressed how God allowed him to go on the mountaintop. Till this day, I love the view of mountains.

They are serene, powerful, and majestic. The life God offered was much more and greater. However the words *you are chosen* haunts me to this day. I find myself running, fearful of being ridiculed, and unworthy.

Years later, now in 2014, I find myself in another situation that led to termination due to telling the truth. This is devastating because I was labeled as displaying misconduct. That's why I can relate to Jesus and the calling of the disciples, which I think was honorable but devastating.

Facing adversity is no easy challenge and doesn't feel good. In my opinion, I've developed over the years and realized this spiritual realm is God's way of communicating.

The Challenge

—∞∞∞—

Eighty-First and Maryland was very significant in my life. Now that God was revealing himself to me, I was somewhat curious and doubtful. So I began testing my spiritual power or gift. I recall asking for a sign from God—that if he were real, to show me a sign. Since this spiritual realm was new to me, my curiosity was peaking. Now my mom always told me if you really want an answer from God, pray in water. So being a daring person, I prayed in bathwater for God to show me a sign that he really existed.

Just to give a visual layout of our apartment and where the bathroom was located: Our bathroom was between the living room and dining room but facing the front door as you walked inside the apartment. Anyway, I'm not sure what night or for how long, but God accommodated my request. This experience happened in a dream, but it seemed so real. I saw myself in the tub, the same way I prayed for this sign, but the only difference was the bathroom door was opened. In reality I don't take a bath or shower with the door open, but as I looked outside the bathroom door into the hallway, I observed this spirit at the entrance door of the apartment. I called my girlfriend's name, *Angie, Angie,* as I hung over the tub slightly. It's funny now, as I recall telling her to stop playing. Once I realized it wasn't her, I whispered to myself, "It's a sign." This spirit was bright and appeared to be in an image of man. It stood tall and upright. I was afraid, particularly since I was in a vulnerable state. In this vision

I remember closing and opening my eyes, and the image was gone. People, I didn't ask for a sign for years after that. I learned you don't challenge or play with the supernatural. There is a spiritual realm among us, but I think we take it lightly.

Bleeding Walls

───❦───

I expressed earlier the uniqueness of our apartment at 81st and Maryland. This apartment had feelings of its own. After a long day at work—I don't recall what day—I entered the apartment as usual, and as I closed the door and walked into the dining room where the creepy chandelier was, I saw the living room walls bleeding. You can only imagine the words in my head. Seeing the walls drenched in blood was indescribable. As I continued looking through the apartment, the bedroom was dripping, as well as the living room, but the dining room was primarily soaked with blood. I took my outerwear off and asked myself, *How can I clean this up before Angie gets home?*

I grabbed a clear bucket of water and a towel to begin cleaning. At the same time, I was fussing and mad because no one would believe this situation. People, this was real! No dream! That's not the crazy part: As I cleaned and realized I was over my head trying to wipe off the walls before Angie got home, right before my eyes this blood started going in reverse. I dropped the towel and visited my neighbor for about thirty minutes to an hour. I told him what had happened, and he refused to come witness it. He expressed how the apartment could have sweated from the radiator heaters and bled onto the wallpaper underneath. I told him, "No! The walls are white." It's funny how people react to the unnatural and try to make logical sense out of situations that are of the spirit world.

Meanwhile, I returned downstairs to the apartment, and Angie was there. I looked at her and she asked, "Why do you look strange?" I told her she wouldn't believe it and I'll wait until she gets comfortable after her hard day at work. She asked, "Why is the bucket here and water on floor?"

Again, I expressed to her that she wouldn't believe this. As she got comfortable, I described to her how the walls were bleeding and it was overwhelming as I tried cleaning up before she got home. At that moment she thought I had been smoking something, and I expressed that no, this really happened. That's why I left the bucket—so she could see the red water. She saw the bucket with red water and agreed with our neighbor John that perhaps there was wallpaper underneath the paint. I disagreed with her and stated, "If that's the case, why did everything go in reverse and back to normal before you came home?" Now that I'm older, I realize that perhaps it wasn't for her to observe; everyone can't handle phenomena of the supernatural.

This experience, I never shared until now; these are events that are not normal conversation. Although I'm sharing these experiences now, I believe God wants me to share these spiritual revelations because we truly are living in the last days. I am mature enough to stand and confirm these events and experiences really happened in this lifetime. I came to the realization that no matter what people may think or say about me and these events, the reality is it happened, and I'm man enough to acknowledge this phenomenon.

Death before Freedom

Over the years, I've learned and believe that God speaks to some of us through dreams. At this point in my life, I'm convinced dreams are warnings and some kind of message depending on what circumstances or experiences individuals are going through.

I've been working for the State of Illinois for about twelve years now, and I've seen lack of accountability and mismanagement at its peak. It's strange—growing up in a religious family teaches us to do the right thing and not lie. However it's not like that in the real world. A person's ethical standards and moral blanket can and will be challenged at some point in their life. Well, I have been confronted with ethical challenges and life changing decisions regarding ethical/moral standards.

Working in Human Resources, you see a lot. However there are policies and procedures in place to help guide those in power to alleviate wrongdoing or corruption; or so I thought. I realized people with titles or power really don't adhere to or follow procedures. Also I learned some people with power are abusive. All of us are blessed with a brain and are capable of doing the right thing but, for whatever reason, it appears we choose to do the opposite of what's right. In learning a job, you always follow directives of upper management. But once a person realizes they are being lied to, that should prompt an individual to research, read, and understand policy and procedures for themselves.

Well, I discovered management wasn't following policy and procedures and when something went wrong, I was being blamed. That wasn't acceptable to me. To make matters worse, I was investigated within two months on the job, as if I were doing something wrong.

This alerted me, and of course I was stern about asking questions and clarification before following any directive. Can you believe, as time passed, I began receiving disciplinary action for not following directives and was considered to be displaying bad conduct? All this stemmed from my continual inquiries and need for clarification.

I prayed about my situation, and it was revealed that I should report this sort of behavior. Reporting this to higher authorities meant I was sacrificing my job due to my beliefs. I had proof, along with policy and procedures, to support that truth. That didn't mean a thing, which messed me up. Retaliations occurred for about three years until I was eventually terminated in July 2014.

During this whole encounter, I recall dreaming about heads floating in a pool of water. What was peculiar about this dream was that these heads were connected by strands of hair. After this, certain individuals retired, moved on suspiciously, and I was eventually terminated.

In another dream during the course of these three years, I saw myself on the edge and had nowhere to go but to fall. I couldn't turn around, and my fate was before me. That was scary because I knew I couldn't fly—but God! God is good. Even while going through this ordeal of performing my job to the best of my ability regardless of the attacks, although I fell off the edge, spiritually I ascended. There was no fear as I saw myself flying. In the past, I would normally awaken from my dreams, but now I walk with faith and believe God is with me.

Before being terminated, I dreamed of a family photo displaying the men in my family. Every son had his father behind him. However I noticed my dad was standing behind my brother and no one was behind me.

I recall feeling bad, but as I looked again, there was this white cloud with the image of God behind me. This picture was spectacular and glorious.

The spirit of God being behind me meant more to me than anything. My son and I drove down south to join the men of the family on Father's Day weekend of this particular year. That's the weekend I broke my finger. My biological dad was very supportive during this misfortune, and it carried over when I was terminated. It was my dad who reminded me that I lost my job due to politics and I had stood my ground in doing what was right even though I was released. That made me feel good; but losing your job for being ethical and labeled for misconduct affects your psyche.

I learned people can be evil and lie with no guilty conscious. Their souls are rotten, and they're spiritually deceased, walking in this world like zombies existing in the matrix. We all die in some way or another; some of us die and become free, while others wander in the land of the living with no direction or conscious. Losing a job that challenges your ethics and morals is devastating, but I believe it freed me to write and release my experiences. I hope and pray that these experiences will bless someone.

Meeting Jesus

Presently, I find myself in transition. I'm terminated from a state job after four terrible years. Management wasn't following policy and procedures in reconciling biweekly payroll entries, and I reported this lack of accountability because I decided not to be the fall guy. Some people might say that I was foolish for doing such a thing; however I was being blamed for many incidents that weren't my fault and being investigated within a month of accepting the job offer. I'm an ethical guy and won't tolerate anyone lying on me. Now I'm terminated, and it's documented as misconduct. Politics at work! Now I'm faced with a new perspective but confused about what direction I should be following.

God blessed me with the gift of poetry or spoken word, which have been sitting dormant for approximately twelve years. I've been published locally and presently am sitting on a poetry collection that I would like to publish. Since I have the time during this transition, I've gathered all my writings and arranged them in different categories. After arranging and reviewing, I have two books I can share with the world. Look at God!

It's possible that my new direction is to utilize my gift and bless someone in this world. With that being said, I have something significant to say and share but was always afraid because of a judgmental society. Maybe it wasn't time to share because God knew I wasn't mature at the time, and I had to learn to disregard what humanity might say about me.

The dreams and experiences I'm about to share are real and truly happened, but from a spiritual perspective. First I want to acknowledge God is real! This experience happened in 1982, while I was attending Chicago Vocational High School. I resided with my dad at the time and didn't believe in God. As far as I was concerned, why believe in something you can't touch, see, or feel?

There was a young lady in my geometry class named Valerie who was a Jehovah's Witness. She was cute. Her eyes were green, and she had a fair complexion. I used to tease her because in my eyes she didn't do anything, was a good girl, but I flirted with her because she was nice and wholesome. One day she just expressed how we would never date because we were different—I was worldly. I recall taking offense and saying some unworldly things due to the fact I was lusting for her. All I remember her saying before our conversation ended: "I will be praying for you because you need to change."

I never knew someone could have that much power; perhaps two or three weeks later I had a nerve-racking but memorable experience. I say it's an experience because I literally awoke from my sleep. I don't recall what day, but I remember sleeping with my bedroom door closed, as I always do, and leaving my radio on at a low volume. Meanwhile on this particular night, I woke up cold. It was so cold, I felt like I was in an ice box. As I turned facing the bedroom door, I noticed a bright light shining. It wasn't your ordinary light; it was like a cloud. Immediately I became frightened and covered my head.

I thought it was a burglar, and I was afraid to yell for help. Eventually I found courage to remove the covers from my head, and the light was gone. This was baffling to me. *I know I'm not crazy*, I thought to myself. I did see a light. Before I could further doubt myself, I heard this voice saying, "I'm Jesus, son of God." I became so frightened that I turned toward the wall and hid my face in fear. All I could think about was how cold I was. My life reflected before me; Jesus knew all that I had done. Let me share something with you, Gangster Disciples: When you display pitchforks, that represents the devil. I had to stop flagging those forks. I was compelled to listen to Jesus as he expressed that that represented the Devil. Also I recall Jesus asking me what I wanted for my birthday. Yeah, I know some of you are saying, "Yeah, right." But it's true. My birthday is April 11th, and was falling on Easter in 1982. Nevertheless I was so afraid that I didn't respond. I don't remember falling asleep or when he departed, but I awoke due to my alarm clock going off. I laid in bed asking myself, *Was Jesus really here?*

I looked at the bedroom door, and it was closed as if it had never happened. But then I noticed my radio was on. During the encounter, I never heard my radio. Before I got out of bed, I noticed a print, as if someone were sitting there. In addition it appeared that I was tucked neatly in the bed. After that I was convinced and had proof.

I went to school that day and saw Valerie. I recall telling her I had something significant to tell her. She was so eager to know, but I expressed to her that it was confusing. I told Valerie all about my experience and she was excited, overjoyed, and who knows what else. I told her it doesn't mean anything, but she stated, "You don't understand or have a clue." We laughed as I told her she had jinxed me. You know, it's funny—I never disrespected or flirted with her after that experience.

This is one of the experiences I have held internally for years as I prepare to share more; and hopefully, somewhere in this world, many will be blessed or can relate to the spiritual realm that exists among us.

Enemies

In this life we experience different things. But I believe we all have something that we have encountered: Enemies! Some of our foes are great and some aren't. It's the year 1991, and now Angie and I are married. We now live at 88th and Stony Island. Both of us are still working and pursuing our educations. Working and attending school is challenging but manageable. We're able to travel a bit and enjoy the luxuries of life. Gas is $1.50 a gallon and twenty-five dollars goes a long way for a weekend extravaganza.

I work in the transit sector, and it's enjoyable due to coworkers I've met over the years. Working in Chicago, especially in a bureaucracy molded by politics and corruption, can easily manipulate and dictate one's ethical behavior. Growing up in a Baptist home, being taught to be honest, and telling the truth have their place but don't necessarily coincide with the realities of some working conditions.

Some of the people I thought were friends were snakes in disguise. This guy I knew managed tuition reimbursement and had the ability to cut checks and adjust the paperwork to reflect what classes employees took as well as the days and hours. I know this because one day this so-called friend brought me a check for about $500 dollars. It looked so legit that even I almost fell in this trap. Meanwhile I asked, "Why am I getting an extra check?" I didn't recall taking this particular class. He had some line but expressed that he couldn't take the check back, and that it's mine. So I said, "Ok."

Before I could walk away, he asked, "What are you going to do for me?"

I asked, "What you mean?"

Now the drama began. He expressed that he had given me the check and I didn't want to show gratitude. I asked, "What you want?" After he said he wanted half the check, I knew something was wrong. I immediately told him that I wasn't giving him anything: "If the check is mine, I will spend it. If not, I'll return it with no problem." The way people will do you is unreal. I held that check for two days and conferred with a payroll supervisor regarding what I should do. After consulting with that supervisor, I had to return the check in order to clear my name. As he stated, "You'll get $500 now." Eventually the company would have caught up with me, and I would have been responsible for the whole amount.

On top of that, this so-called friend followed me for about a week. Today I am very careful about whom I surround myself with. It's hard to trust; you never know people's intentions.

After that incident I remember having various dreams that consisted of dogs and snakes. The dream that stands out significantly was about the snake. It was so long and took about six or eight people to carry it out. I remember the fear I felt as I smoothly moved out of the way. My grandfather was alive during this time, and I shared the dream with him. Granddaddy said, "You have enemies." We laughed and joked about it but deep inside I was asking myself, *Why?*

I don't cause any harm and try to be nice and cordial toward those I meet. Who am I?

I've learned that sometimes people can take your kindness for weakness or some sort of naivete. Also being ethical is challenging. It's not easy doing the right thing, because you eventually get labeled. Being labeled isn't nice, but over the years I've matured enough to be comfortable with myself. I don't worry about what people say about me; God made me this way, and I love myself enough to be different and stand alone, if I have to.

Another among Us

The supernatural has a way of making itself known and can sometimes leave us questioning our sanity. Before moving from 81st and Maryland, Angie and I experienced this spirit that wanted us to know it was real. One morning we both were getting ready for work. We listened to the radio every morning, getting the news and weather as usual. This particular morning I heard this abnormal breathing on the radio. I thought it was the radio personality, at that time, but the breathing was absurd and obnoxious. It sounded like someone breathing heavily after having sex or perhaps someone who had asthma. What was peculiar about this experience was that it was early in the morning and wasn't a dream. We were awake. I thought if I turned the radio down, it would stop. That wasn't the case: When I turned the volume down, the breathing was louder. When I turned the volume back up, it was normal. I asked Angie to come into the living room and watch this. She heard the breathing, but when I turned the volume down, it got louder. We turned the radio off, and I remember saying that the stereo my mom bought for me was possessed, and I got mad. I said, "Whoever you are, you got to go; we don't want you here." I immediately got dressed and left for work. That particular incident never happened again.

We take a lot of things for granted. So many things happen that we can't explain, and some people disregard them.

People are uncomfortable and don't want to talk about the spiritual realm.

Instead we want to characterize or label people as crazy or schizophrenic because they are tuned in to a world that isn't visual but in which the presence of another is prevalent. In some cases we can hear unseen spirits and smell them. It's unfortunate—no matter what religion or faith we proclaim, we fail to acknowledge the existence of the spiritual realm through the naked eye.

Made in United States
Cleveland, OH
13 August 2025

19196644R00062